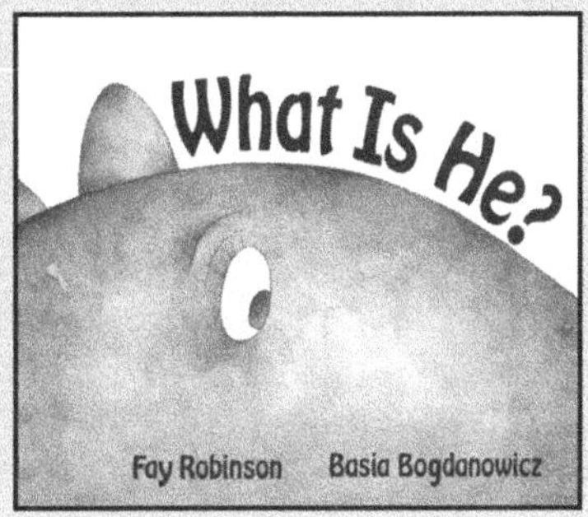

Walkthrough

Read the title of the book.

'What is he?'

Point out the question mark.

What do you think he is?

What part of him can you see?

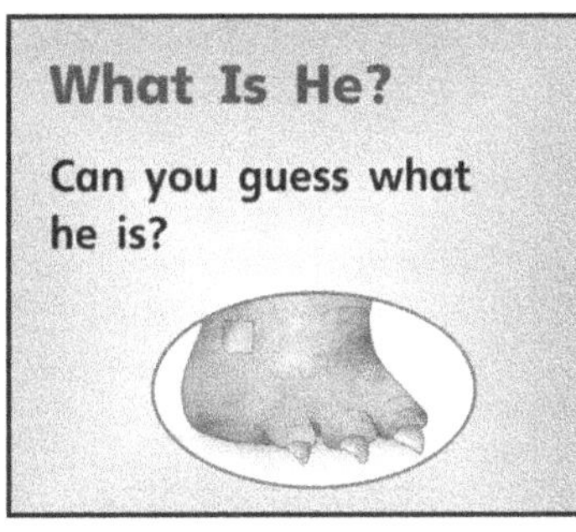

Walkthrough

This is the back cover – let's read the blurb together.

'Can you guess what he is?'

(Prompt for suggestions.)

What part of him can you see in the picture?

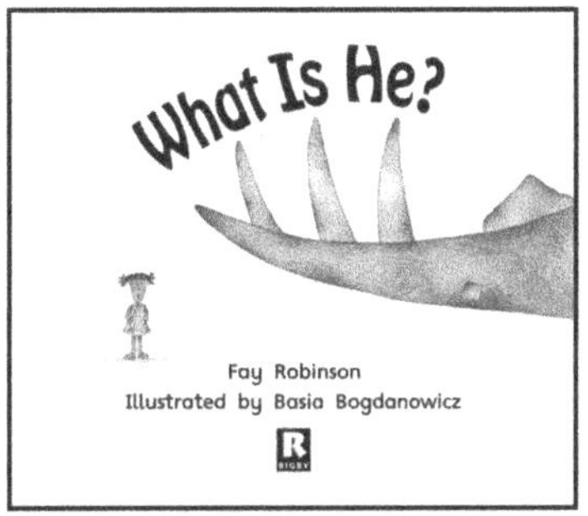

Walkthrough

This is the title page.

Let's read the title again.

This is another part of the animal – do you have any other ideas?

Read the names of the author and illustrator to the children.

This is the logo of the publisher.

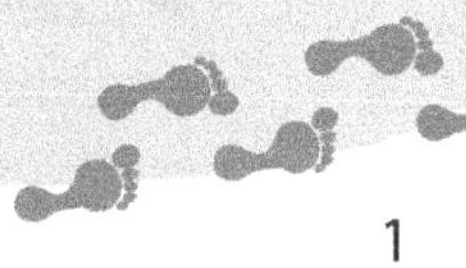

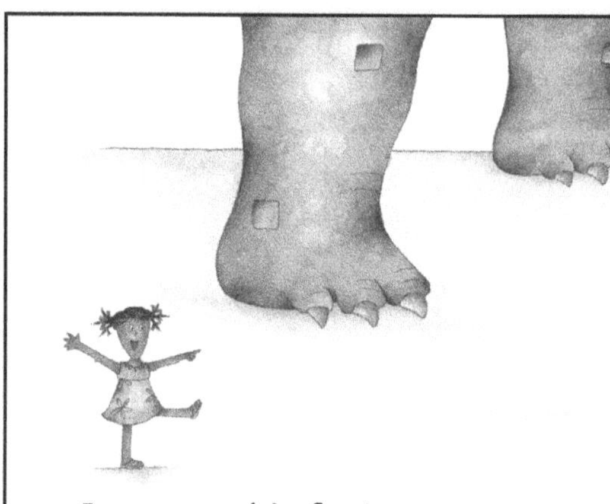

👁 Observe and Prompt

Word Recognition

- Check the children are reading 'can' using their decoding skills. Can they sound out and blend c-a-n all through the word?

- Check the children are reading 'feet' using their decoding skills. Help them with the 'ee' sound if they struggle.

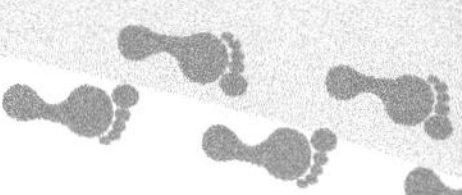

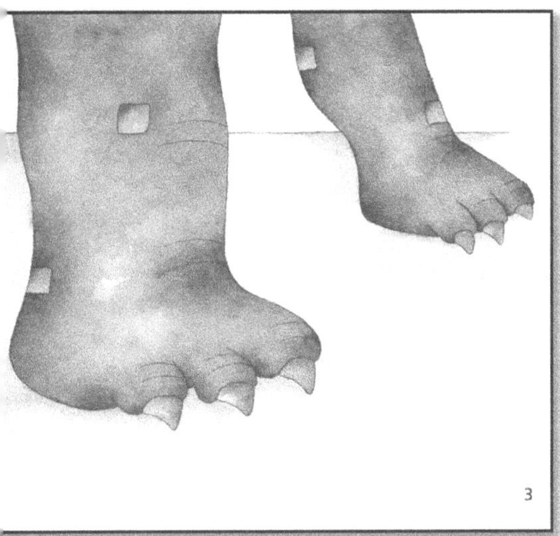

Observe and Prompt

Language Comprehension

- Ask the children what the girl can see.
- Ask the children what the girl says.
- Do the children know who these feet belong to?

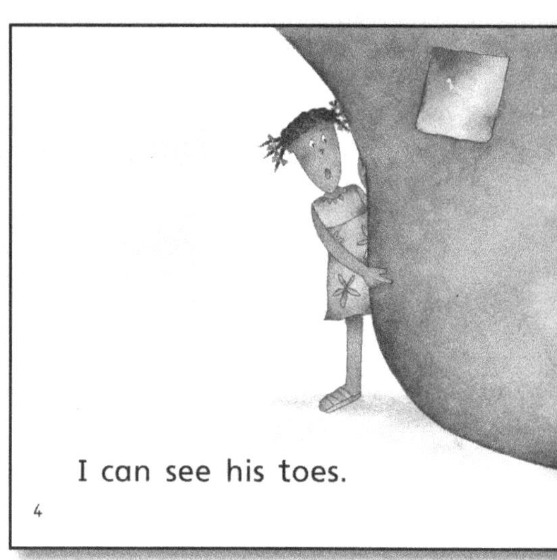

Observe and Prompt

Word Recognition

- Check the children can read the words 'see' and 'his'. (These are sight words – words likely to be in their store of familiar words.)

- The word 'toes' may not be decodable for the children at this stage. If they have difficulty, ask them if they recognise the initial letter and sound – 't'. Then tell them this word and model the reading of it for them.

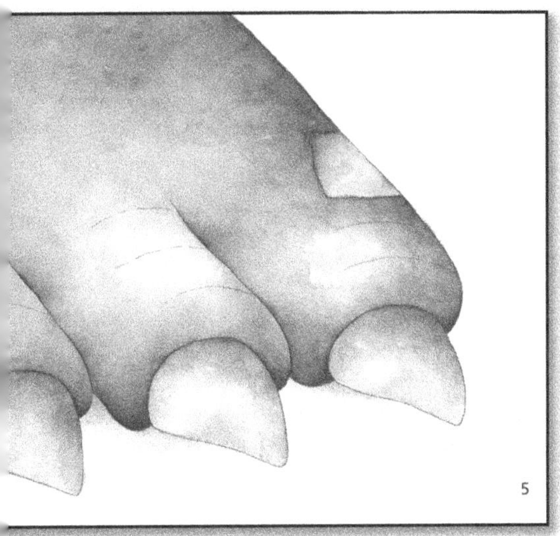

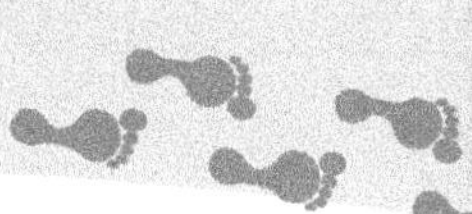

Observe and Prompt

Language Comprehension

- Ask the children what the girl can see now.
- How do the children think the girl feels?
- How can they tell?

Which part of the animal can the girl see?

What do you think he is?

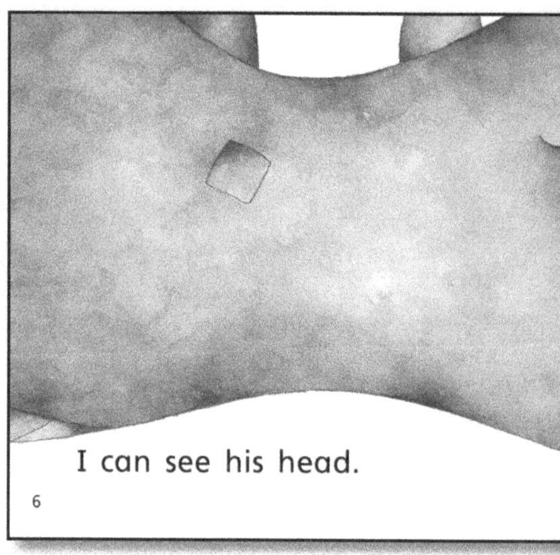

Observe and Prompt

Word Recognition

- Check the children can read the sight word 'I' confidently.
- The word 'head' may not be decodable for the children at this stage. Tell them this word and model the reading of it for them.

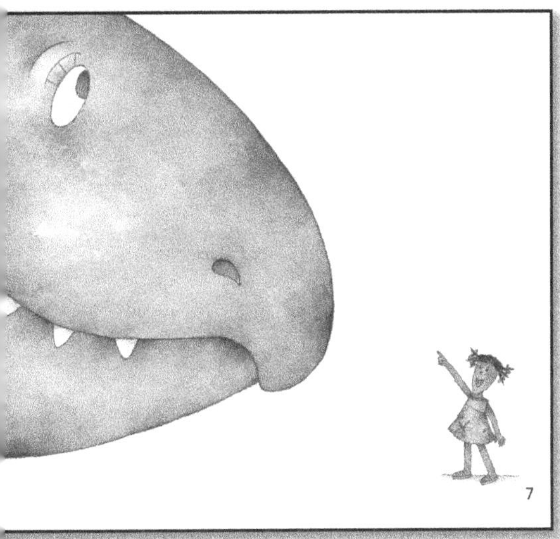

Language Comprehension

- Ask the children what the girl is saying now.
- Can the children guess what animal he is?

Walkthrough

What part of the animal can the girl see?

What is she holding up?

What might this be for?

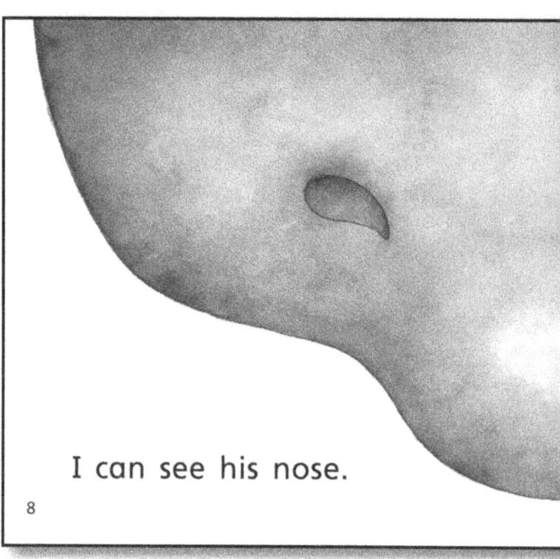

 **Observe and Prompt**

Word Recognition

- If the children have difficulty with the word 'nose', ask them if they recognise the initial letter and sound – 'n'. Then tell them the word and model the reading of it for them.

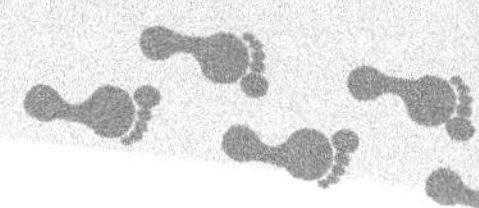

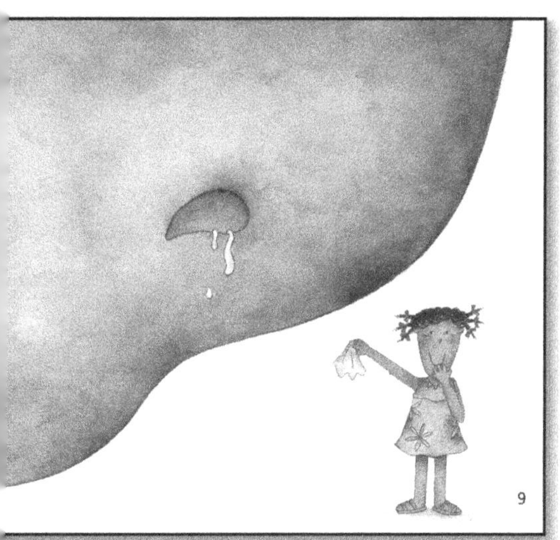

![eye icon] **Observe and Prompt**

Language Comprehension

- Ask the children what the girl can see now.
- Ask the children what the girl might be thinking.
- What else do the children think the girl can see?

Walkthrough

Which part of the animal can the girl see now?

What do you think he is?

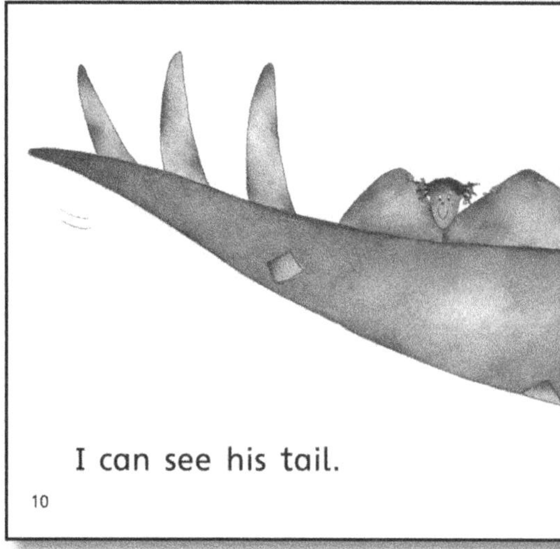

Observe and Prompt

Word Recognition

- The word 'tail' may not be decodable for the children at this stage. Tell them this word and model the reading of it for them.

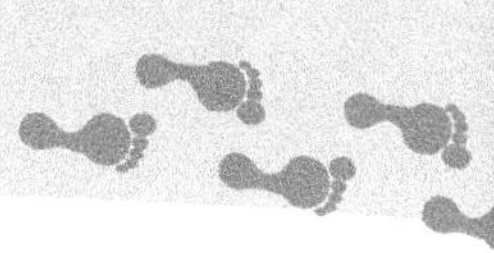

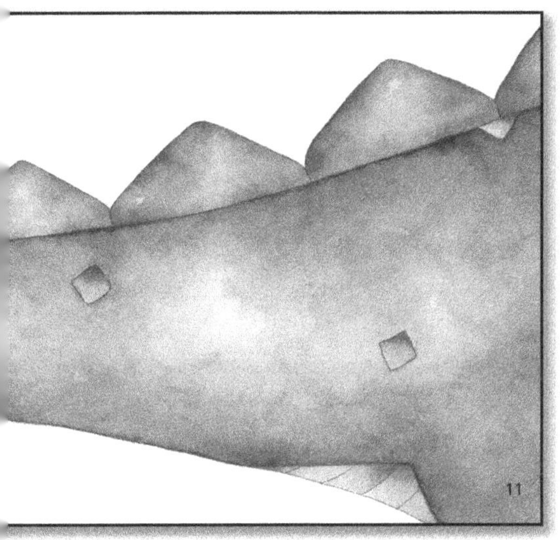

Observe and Prompt

Language Comprehension

- Ask the children which part of the animal the girl can see now.
- Do the children think it is a big animal?

Walkthrough

What noise is the animal making?

What might the girl say?

 **Observe and Prompt**

Word Recognition

- The word 'hear' will not be decodable for the children at this stage. Tell them this word and model the reading of it for them.

- If children have difficulty with the word 'roar', ask them if they recognise the initial letter and sound – 'r'. Then model the reading of this word for them.

- Check the children read 'him' and not 'his', using their decoding skills.

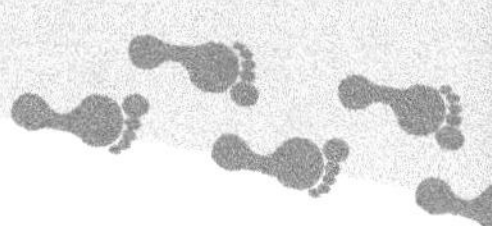

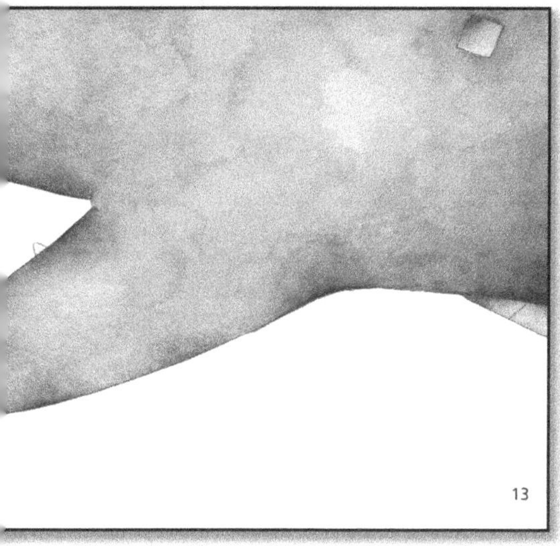

13

Observe and Prompt

Language Comprehension

- Check the children understand what is happening in the story now.

- Ask the children if the roar is loud or quiet. How can they tell?

- Prompt for expressive reading.

Walkthrough

What do you think he is?

Do you think the girl knows?

 ## Observe and Prompt

Word Recognition

- Check the children are reading the words independently with confidence.

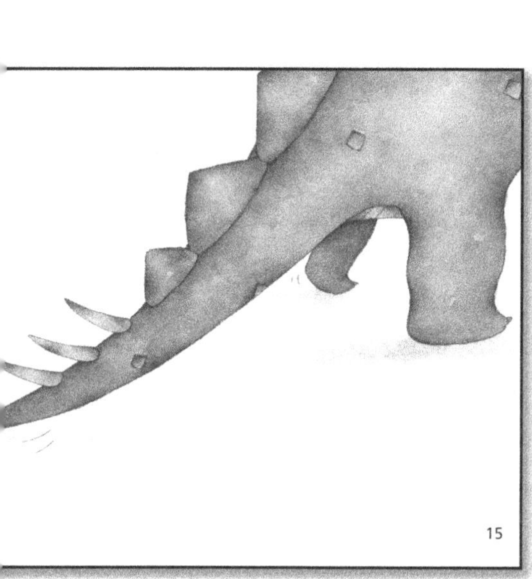

 **Observe and Prompt**

Language Comprehension

- Check the children understand the dots (ellipsis) and model quick page turning.
- What do the children think the girl can see?

 **Observe and Prompt**

Word Recognition

- Check the children can read the sight word 'a' with confidence.

- The word 'dinosaur' will not be decodable for the children at this stage. Ask them if they recognise the initial sound and letter – 'd'. Then model the reading of the word for them.

Language Comprehension

- Ask the children what it was that the girl could see.

- How does the girl feel? How can they tell?

- Would the children be afraid of the dinosaur?